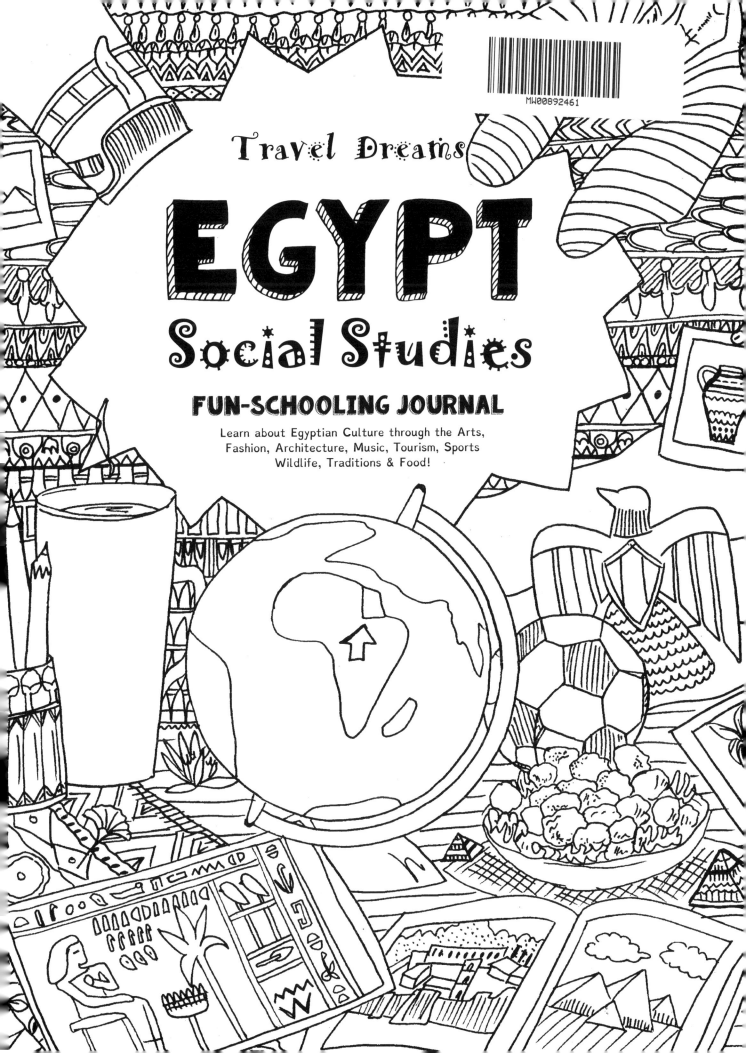

Travel Dreams

EGYPT

Social Studies

FUN-SCHOOLING JOURNAL

Learn about Egyptian Culture through the Arts,
Fashion, Architecture, Music, Tourism, Sports
Wildlife, Traditions & Food!

To hear traditional music from this country listen to

Travel Dreams
Geography

AROUND THE WORLD
IN 14 SONGS

Search for Amazon Product Number: B072C2QXJS

Around the world in **14** songs is a delightful musical tour of the world. Adults and children will enjoy these original instrumental songs that reflect the authentic style of music that originated on all six major continents. Travel to the rhythm and melody of traditional instruments, and enjoy the fun-filled tunes.

The musical journey begins in Ireland, sweeps across Europe, dances through Asia, Africa and then soars over the ocean to Australia and the Caribbean! After an exciting night at a Smoky Mountain bluegrass festival you will enjoy a siesta in Mexico and finally land in Brazil where you will join the festa in Rio-De-Janeiro.

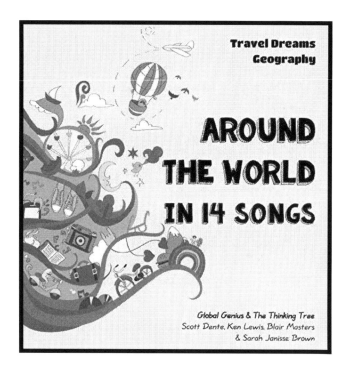

Music has never been more fun... or educational!

Travel Dreams
EGYPT
FUN-SCHOOLING
JOURNAL

An Adventurous Approach
Social Studies

Learn about Egyptian Culture Through the Arts,
Fashion, Architecture, Music, Tourism, Sports,
Wildlife, Traditions & Food!

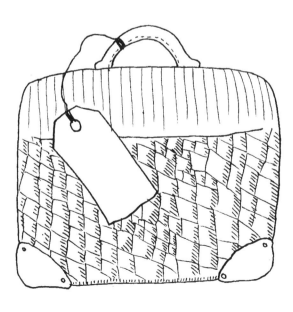

Tunis

Egypt

Travel Dreams
EGYPT
FUN-SCHOOLING
Journal

Name:

Date:

Contact Information:

About Me:

Let's Learn!

Topics & Activities You Can Explore With This Curriculum:

- Ethnic Cooking
- Travel
- History of Interesting Places
- How People Live
- Tourism
- Transportation
- Wildlife and Natural Wonders
- Cultural Traditions
- Natural Disasters

- Famous and Interesting People
- Missionary Stories
- Scientific Discoveries
- Fashion
- Architecture
- Plants
- Animals
- Maps
- Language

EGYPT

EGYPT

Travel Dreams Fun-School Journal
You are going to learn about Egypt

Teacher & Parent To-Do List:

- Plan a trip to Egypt or just plan a trip to the library or local bookstore.
- Download Google Earth so your child can zoom in and learn more!
- Choose online videos about Egypt so your child can learn about culture, food, tourism, traditions and history.
- Be prepared to help your child choose an ethnic recipe and shop for the ingredients.

Go to the Library or Bookstore to Pick Out:

- Books about Egypt
- One Atlas or Book of Maps
- One Colorful Cookbook with Recipes from Egypt

DRAW THE COVER OF YOUR BOOKS!

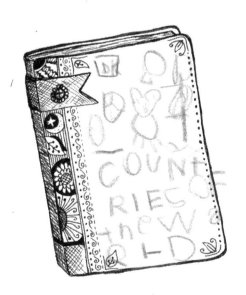

COLOR IN EGYPT ON THE MAP

Zoom into Egypt using Google Earth, and explore the wonders
of this amazing country!

LABEL THE MAP
Add 15 Interesting Things to this Map!

Write or Draw
Use your Library Books

Popular Foods:	Traditional Clothing:
Draw the Flag:	**A Quote or Proverb:**
A Historic Event:	**A Famous Landmark:**

LEARNING TIME

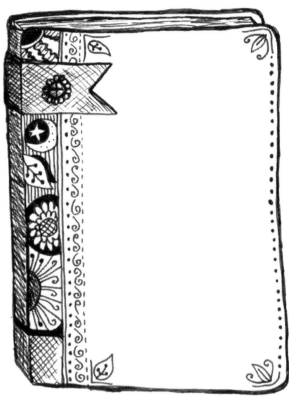

READ A BOOK AND WATCH A VIDEO ABOUT FOOD IN EGYPT:

BOOK TITLE:_____
_____
VIDEO TITLE: _____
_____
_____

What did you learn?

_____
_____
_____
_____
_____
_____

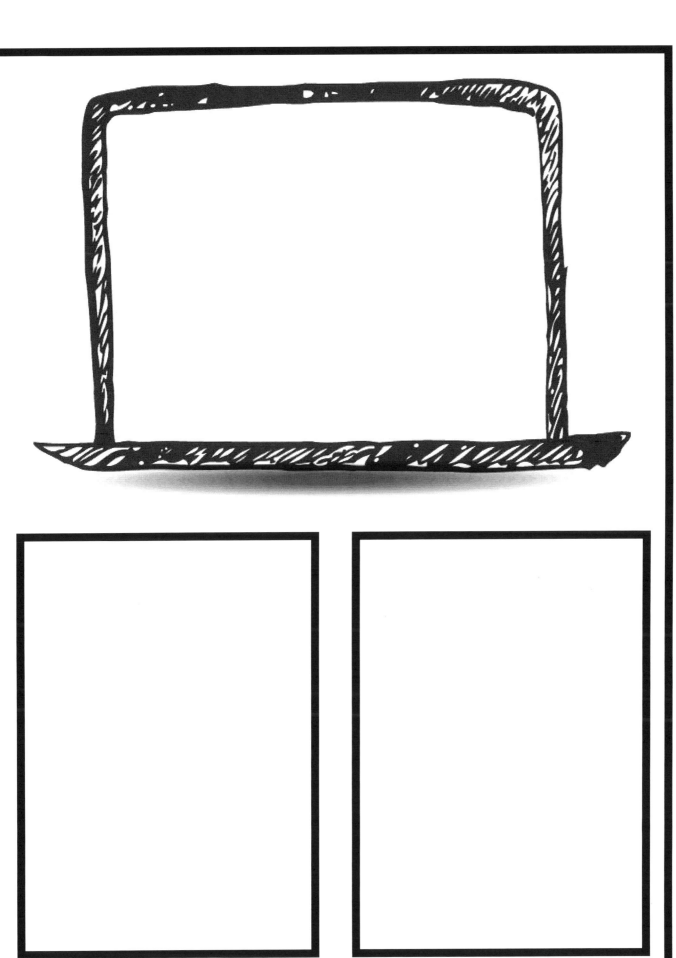

EGYPTIAN CUISINE

What do Egyptians love to eat?

Can you list 5 of the most popular Egyptian dishes?

1. _____
2. _____
3. _____
4. _____
5. _____
6.

Draw your favorite Egyptian food

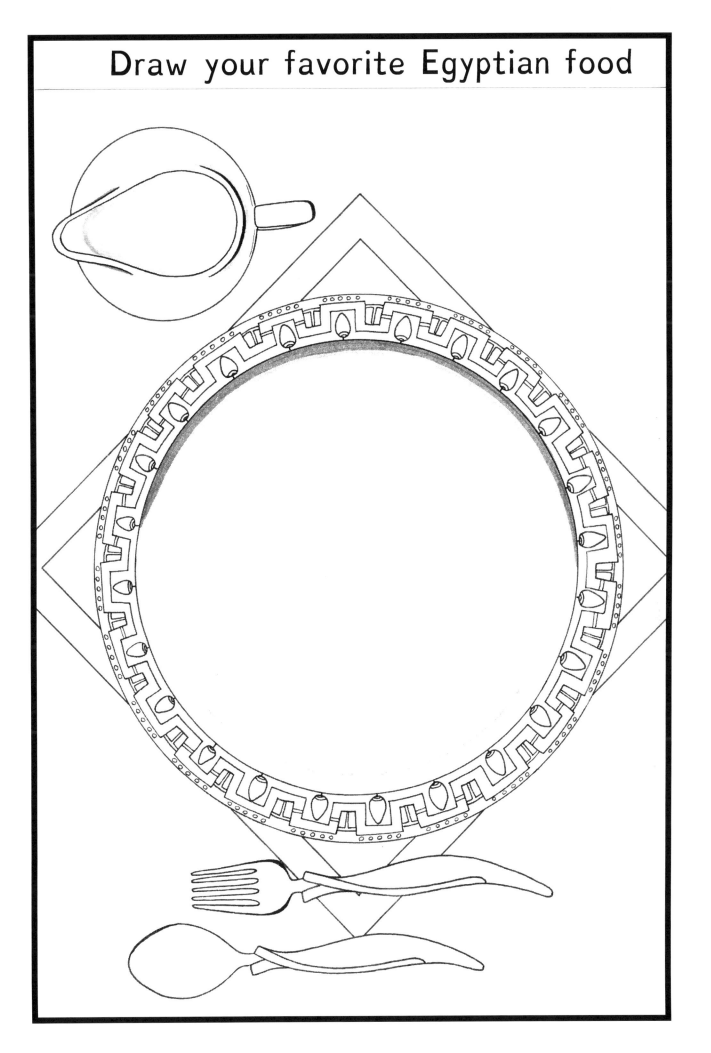

Find a Recipe From
EGYPT
TITLE:

Ingredients:

---------------------   ---------------------

---------------------   ---------------------

---------------------   ---------------------

---------------------   ---------------------

---------------------   ---------------------

Instructions:

Step by Step Food Prep:

1	2
3	4
5	6

DRAW THE FOOD THAT YOU PREPARED!

RATE THE RESULTS! 1, 2, 3, 4, 5

Color the words that best describe your food:

DELICIOUS

YUMMY

TASTY

GREAT

DELIGHTFUL

OKAY

BLAH!

GROSS

YUCKY

DISGUSTING

STINKY

ICKY

What to Do in Egypt

Create a **COMIC STRIP** showing your dream adventure!

LEARNING TIME

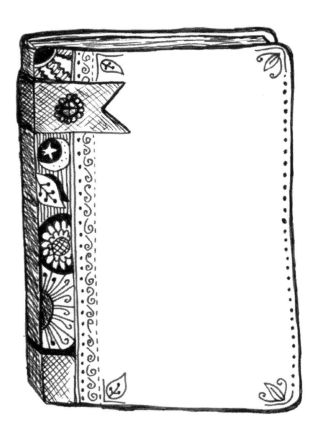

READ A BOOK AND WATCH A VIDEO ABOUT A FAMOUS PERSON

BOOK TITLE:_____
_____
VIDEO TITLE: _____
_____
_____

Write 3 Interesting Biography Facts

_____
_____
_____
_____
_____
_____

All About Style
EGYPT
Fashion in the City

_____

_____

_____

MODERN STYLES
Draw yourself dressed like a stylish Egyptian :

Color The Traditional Costume:

Trace and color this traditional Female Egyptian costume

Trace and color this traditional Male Egyptian costume

EGYPTIAN HISTORY

Write about a Historic Event

_____

_____

_____

_____

_____

_____

_____

_____

_____

_____

_____

_____

_____

_____

_____

LEARNING TIME

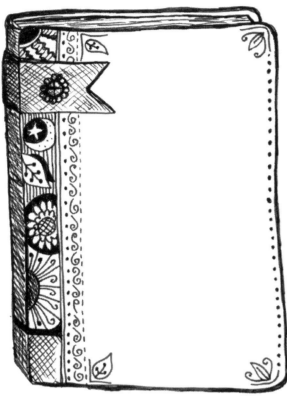

READ A BOOK AND WATCH A VIDEO ABOUT NATURE & WILDLIFE

BOOK TITLE:_____
_____
VIDEO TITLE: _____
_____
_____

Notes:
_____
_____
_____
_____
_____
_____

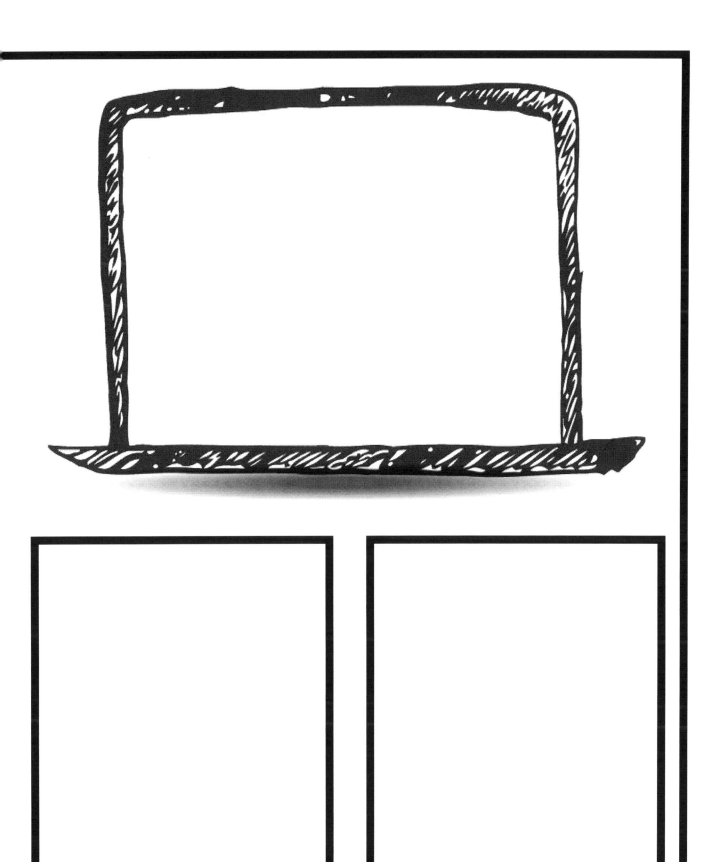

WHaT ANiMaLS LiVe iN Egypt? CaN yoU LiSt teN?

1. _____
2. _____
3. _____
4. _____
5. _____
6. _____
7. _____
8. _____
9. _____
10. _____

Draw each of the animals

PLANTS IN EGYPT

Can you list ten flowers or trees found in Egypt?

1. _____
2. _____
3. _____
4. _____
5. _____
6. _____
7. _____
8. _____
9. _____
10. _____

Draw each of the plants

HISTORY OF MUSIC IN EGYPT

Write about a famous Egyptian musician;

_____

_____
_____
_____
_____
_____
_____

What instrument did he/she play?

_____

Can you draw it?

A NATIONAL INSTRUMENT

To hear traditional music from this country listen to
Travel Dreams Geography—Around the World in **14** Songs

Track Number & Song Name:
06-Egypt - Thieves of Cairo

EGYPTIAN ART & ENTERTAINMENT

Read a book or watch a documentary about art and entertainment in Egypt

Write down 5 interesting things you learned :

1._____
_____

2._____
_____

3._____
_____

4._____
_____

5._____
_____

Draw or doodle in Egyptian Style

Write doWN a quote or a Lyric From a Famous Egyptian poem or Song

_____

_____

_____

_____

_____

_____

_____

_____

_____

_____

_____

_____

_____

HISTORY OF TRANSPORTATION IN EGYPT

Find 3 interesting Facts about Egyptian transportation

1. _____
_____
_____

2. _____
_____
_____

3. _____
_____
_____

Use your imagination and add something to this picture

Write a short story about this picture

_____

_____

_____

_____

_____

_____

_____

_____

_____

EGYPTIAN INVENTIONS

Read a book or watch a documentary about your favorite Egyptian inventor:

_____

Write down 5 interesting things about his/her life:

1. _____

_____

2. _____

_____

3. _____

_____

4. _____

_____

5. _____

_____

Write down 3 Egyptian inventions that changed the world:

1. _____

2. _____

3. _____

Draw your Favorite Egyptian invention

EGYPTIAN SPORTS

Read a book or watch a documentary about your favorite Egyptian Sport:

_____

Write down 5 interesting things about this sport

1._____
_____

2._____
_____

3._____
_____

4._____
_____

5._____
_____

DraW your Favorite Egyptian Sport

EGYPTIAN HOMES
Write about a Family tradition in Egypt

_____

_____

_____

_____

EGYPTIAN TRADITIONS
Draw some traditional Egyptian décor elements

Trace & Color
A TRADITIONAL EGYPTIAN HOME

Design Your Own
EGYPTIAN HOME

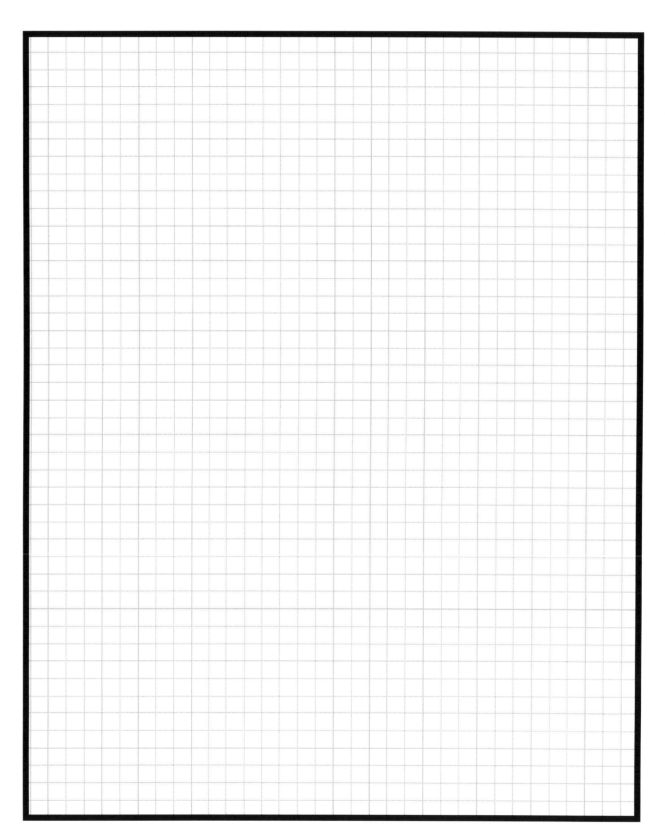

FiND AND COLOr iN THe HiDDeN ObjectS

LEARNING TIME

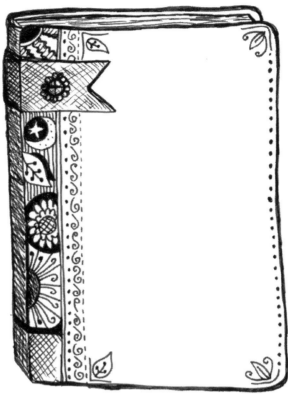

READ A BOOK AND WATCH A VIDEO ABOUT TOURISM & TRAVEL

BOOK TITLE:_____
_____
VIDEO TITLE: _____
_____
_____

Notes:
_____
_____
_____
_____
_____
_____

PLAN A TRIP TO THE CAPITAL OF EGYPT

Who are you going with?

_____

What are you taking with you?

_____

How long is your trip?

_____

What do you want to see or visit?

_____

PLAN YOUR TRIP

What to Do in Cairo

Five Things to Know
when Traveling to
EGYPT

1 _____

2 _____

3 _____

4 _____

5 _____

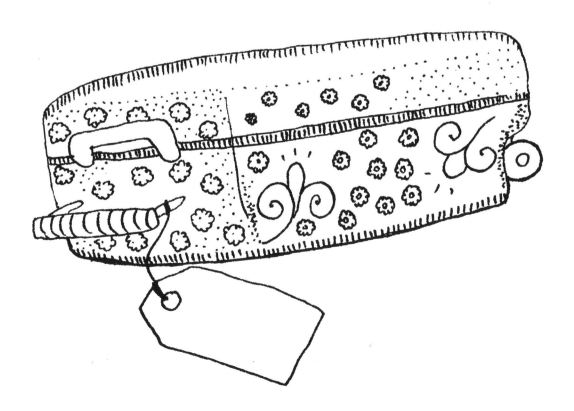

What to Say

Create a COMIC STRIP using six Egyptian words or phrases:

CREATIVE WRITING

Write a story about an imaginary trip to Egypt

Illustrate your Story

Do it Yourself
HOMESCHOOL
JOURNALS
BY THE THINKING TREE, LLC

Made in the USA
Las Vegas, NV
19 September 2021